.gnato,   per te ho vin_to!

due soli
con Sordina

D0160526

B Andantino ♪ = 116

p

Solo *col canto*

con espressione

Ce _ le-ate A_i_

Solo

ppp dolce

_vi _ na,..... mi. _ sti

con Sordina

con Sordina

con Sordina

pizz.

p
pizz.

p
pizz.

p
pizz..

The Tenors

BLACK DOG MUSIC LIBRARY

The Tenors

Luigi Alva • Carlo Bergonzi • Jussi Björling • José Carreras
Enrico Caruso • Franco Corelli • Giuseppe di Stefano
Plàcido Domingo • Nicolai Gedda • Beniamino Gigli
Alfredo Kraus • John McCormack • Lauritz Melchior
Luciano Pavarotti • Richard Tucker

TEXT BY DAVID FOIL

BLACK DOG & LEVENTHAL PUBLISHERS
NEW YORK

Copyright ©1995 Black Dog & Leventhal Publishers Inc.

All rights reserved. No part of this book may be reproduced in any form or by
any electronic or mechanical means, including information storage and retrieval
systems, without the written permission of the copyright holder.

The enclosed compact disc compilation ℗1995 CEMA Special Markets.
Product of CEMA Special Markets, a division of Capitol Records, Inc.,
1750 N. Vine St., Los Angeles, CA 90028

All rights of the producer and owner of the work reproduced on the compact disc
are reserved. Unauthorized copying, hiring, lending, public performance, and
broadcasting of the compact disc are prohibited.

Published by
Black Dog & Leventhal Publishers Inc.
151 West 19th Street
New York, NY 10011

Distributed by
Workman Publishing Company
708 Broadway
New York, NY 10003

Designed by Martin Lubin and Allison Russo

Special thanks to Judith Dupré

Book manufactured in Hong Kong

ISBN: 1-884822-40-1

FOREWORD

*O*ne of the most beloved sounds we hear is that of the tenor's voice.

From Mozart to Puccini, from Enrico Caruso to Luciano Pavarotti, the world has praised with thunderous ovations the brilliance and beauty of the sound the tenor makes. In this volume you will be able to read and learn about the world's great tenors; you will better understand the importance and beauty of their work; and you can enjoy and listen to the music as you read.

Play the compact disc included on the inside front cover of this book and follow along with the musical commentary and analysis.

Enjoy this book and enjoy the music.

The Tenors

*Franco Corelli in the title role
of* Andrea Chénier.

"What is this life?"

Franco Corelli threw out this rhetorical question in a 1976 interview in *Newsweek*, after describing what it felt like to be in the midst of his spectacular career as the most dashing tenor in opera. "I have always been afraid," Corelli confessed. "I wasn't born to be a singer. In the beginning, I didn't have the high C so I was afraid. Then I did have the B and the C but was afraid I would lose them. Sometimes I get up in the morning and the voice doesn't answer. If I'm on holiday and not singing I worry if it's still there. I tape every performance. I then spend three hours listening to the tapes. I am exhausted. I need rest but I can't sleep. If the performance was good I can't sleep for joy. If not, I can't sleep for despair. What is this life?"

It is the life of a tenor. While other tenors may be better able to face the inevitable fluctuations in their careers—the unresolved anguish led Corelli to retire while he was still in superlative voice—they all know what Corelli meant. The tenor is the highest natural male voice. It asks more of a singer than any other category of the singing voice. A tenor must have not only a naturally attractive "instrument" in his throat that is inclined to higher singing, he must develop and support it correctly with breath so that it can deliver powerfully and with beauty in an area of the voice that for men is completely fabricated. Basses and baritones sing, for the most part, in an area (or register) in which the mature male

A triumphant Luciano Pavarotti.

voice is comfortable. The same is true of women, whether they are sopranos, mezzo-sopranos, or contraltos. But the tenor voice must reach up, up, up into thin air, to create and shape a sound while keeping it perfectly within the singer's control. It is the equivalent of a high-wire act. Regardless of how practiced and secure a singer is, the risks every time are enormous.

But so are the rewards. Just listen to a live recording of one of Corelli's stage performances. The barely contained passion in his singing seems to verge on hysteria but produces a thing of mesmerizing beauty. The ovations are thunderous. Being a tenor is, at its best, like being an Olympic athlete or a rock star—but there are no microphones, roadies, or sound mixers to make him sound like a god. Just two little vibrating folds of throat tissue, the air passing over them, and all the will he can muster to sing with style and on pitch.

It wasn't always this strenuous. The tenor voice had been around for centuries before it came into its own as a heroic vocal instrument in the nineteenth century. Tenor, derived from the Latin *tenere*, meaning "to hold," came to be applied to the middle vocal range in traditional three-voice ensembles in medieval and Renaissance music —the part that held long notes to which alto and bass voices were added. When opera materialized in Italy in the early seventeenth century, tenors were given important roles. (Giulio Caccini, one of the most important early opera composers, was himself a tenor.) That changed with the rising popularity of the *castrato* singer, a male castrated before puberty so that his voice never "broke" but remained in the soprano or alto register, supported by the stamina of a physically mature man. This barbaric but fascinating

Gaetano Donizetti

practice dominated opera for most of the eighteenth century. The wild popularity of the greatest *castrati*—Caffarelli, Farinelli, Guadagni, and Senesino—made them the glamorous new stars of opera. In time the shatteringly brilliant sound of the *castrati* lost its appeal.

The tenor returned to prominence in opera in the latter half of the eighteenth century. Mozart wrote extensively for the tenor voice, and might have written even more had the decision to cast certain voice roles not depended on the quality of the tenors available to him. Opera at that time was something created for a single, usually festive, occasion, with little thought of the work's entering a repertory. Mozart would never have insisted —as Richard Wagner did a century later—that tenors struggle to live up to the specific demands of his music. He simply worked with the skills of the artists at his disposal.

As opera entered the Romantic age, the tenor voice was a far different instrument from the one we know today. The range itself was basically the same, usually within two octaves between C and the A just below the note notoriously known as the high C. However, everything above the range of tones that resonate naturally in the chest was sung in a "head," or reinforced falsetto, voice.

All this changed in 1837, when the French tenor Gilbert Duprez created a sensation during a performance of Rossini's *William Tell* at the Paris Opéra by singing a high C in full chest voice. Rossini himself was repulsed by this startling sound—he compared it to the sound of a capon being beheaded—and many agreed that it was ugly and unappealing. But this brilliant new sound was daring, undeniably thrilling, and other tenors strove to learn how to take high Cs from the chest. At the same time, the nature of opera began to undergo radical changes.

The decorative singing required in most of the operas of Bellini, Rossini, and Gaetano Donizetti called for a style now known as *bel canto*, "beautiful singing." These operas, viewed as vehicles for great singers, were shaped specifically to their needs. The emphasis shifted in the 1840s, when the two greatest opera composers of the Romantic age hit their stride— Italy's Giuseppe Verdi and Germany's Richard Wagner. Though each had a very different vision of the opera, both wrote works in which the composer dominated. Singers would now have to arrange their techniques to meet the demands of the score instead of vice versa. Tenors were given more strenuous assignments. It was more than a matter of high notes. What made these new roles so demanding was the stamina and power required to deliver this vigorous, sometimes fierce new music over the sound of a greatly expanded orchestra.

Richard Wagner

Giuseppe Verdi

All of these changes led to the classification of the various kinds of tenor voices—the naïve country-boy hero of Bellini's *La Sonnambula*, for instance, requires a sound far different from that of the passionate, heroic Manrico in Verdi's *Il Trovatore*. Singers, teachers, impresarios, conductors, and composers began to think of tenors in specific ways. The *lirico*, or lyric, tenor is the lightest of the voice divisions. Among lyric tenors is a special type, *tenore di grazia* (tenor of grace), describing a voice that is capable of great flexibility and easy access to high notes. The middleweight voice is the *lirico-spinto*, or lyric-dramatic, tenor. The Italian word *spinto* means "pushed," suggesting here that an essentially lyric voice is being pushed into heavier and more demanding repertoire. A slightly more powerful designation within the lyric-dramatic range is the *tenore di forza* (tenor of force), which usually refers to the heroic roles in late *bel canto* and French operas. The heaviest tenor voice of all is the *tenore robusto* or *heldentenor* (heroic tenor), which has a muscular sound and an almost baritonal quality. The basic span of notes required of the tenor is about the same throughout all classifications of the voice. A key factor in defining these voice types is the range of musical notes in relation to the voice, which is called the *tessitura*, or texture. The tessitura in a lyric tenor's aria, for instance, might be higher. The tessitura in an aria for a heroic tenor might be lower, even though the singer might be required to sing a high C. For example, in the role of Siegmund, the tenor hero of Wagner's *Die Walküre*, the actual notes are not much higher than those a baritone might sing. The highest note Siegmund sings is an A, which should be an easy task for any tenor. The bulk of the role lies lower, however, where it must be sung against the sound of a huge, richly deployed orchestra. It requires unusual baritonal strength, which lyric voices generally do not have, and also demands that the tenor have As that are penetrating and beautiful.

The matter of high notes, particularly the high C, is a nightmare for many tenors. Some tenors simply are "high note" singers, and some are not. Luciano Pavarotti has always had high notes naturally; Plàcido Domingo, like Enrico Caruso, has to work to produce the highest ones. Caruso was so fearful of the high C in Rodolfo's aria "*Che gelida manina*" in *La Bohème* that he convinced Puccini to allow him to transpose it a half-step lower. Puccini concluded that he

Lauritz Melchior exemplifies the Wagnerian **heldentenor.**

Plàcido Domingo

would rather hear Caruso sing the aria beautifully than sing it paralyzed by the knowledge that he had to reach a high C. "Top notes are like goals in football," Pavarotti told Helena Matheopoulos in *Divo*, her book of interviews with great male singers. "If you can do them, fine. If not, no matter. You can still be a great singer without the high C. Caruso didn't have it. Neither did [Tito] Schipa. Schipa didn't even have a particularly beautiful voice. But he was a great singer. He had something twenty times more important than high notes: a great line."

Line refers to the way the singer shapes the music within the tempo prescribed by the conductor. It is perhaps the defining mark of a truly great singer. It is one of Domingo's most eloquent gifts. Pavarotti also has a sovereign command of line. That is why, in the 1994 "Three Tenors" concerts, he could sing a phrase from a well-worn pop song such as "Moon River" and make it sound poetically beautiful, even though his Italian accent was sometimes comical.

Diction and a grasp of languages are important, too, and the most refined singers master several languages in order to illuminate their singing. Until the 1970s, singers in many provincial European opera houses had to sing in the local tongue. In Germany, for instance, Italian opera was performed in German, and Verdi's *La Forza del Destino* became *Der*

Macht das Schicksals. Today, operas are usually performed in the language in which they were written. Language has a powerful impact on the delicate balance a tenor must maintain. The rich, pungent vowels and fluid line of Italian have a vastly different texture than the nasal vowels and diphthongs of French. German and English are more angular-sounding, while Russian, with its "swallowed" vowels, is a complete departure from Eurocentric languages.

The labels *lirico*, *lirico-spinto*, and *tenore robusto* frequently overlap. Tenors freely violate the designations, though Germany's regional opera houses adhere rigidly to the notorious *fach* system, in which voices are pigeonholed (and contracts signed) according to specific qualities. But most singers are free to explore the repertoire that best suits their voices. Alfredo Kraus is perhaps the best modern example of the *tenore di grazia*, yet he has made a specialty of lyric-dramatic roles—Hoffmann in Offenbach's *Les contes d'Hoffmann* and Roméo in Gounod's *Roméo et Juliette*. Plàcido Domingo, essentially a lyric-dramatic tenor, has triumphed in recent years in such heroic roles as Otello, Lohengrin, and Parsifal. One of the chief reasons modern tenors may opt for a range of roles is the remarkable career of Enrico Caruso.

Caruso emerged from Italy at the turn of the twentieth century, a defining moment for modern singing. Wagner's music-dramas were then entering the repertoire, and the cause of Italian opera had passed from Verdi to a new generation that practiced an even more passionate style called *verismo*, meaning "realism." The ardent musings of Bellini's tenors were replaced by the gut-wrenching passions of Puccini's and Mascagni's. Caruso was the first tenor to close the gap convincingly between the lyric and dramatic styles. Those who heard him sing testify to the sheer splendor of his voice, to its warm and compelling sound, but also to its baritonal foundation. Here was a tenor who, it seemed, could do it all superbly well, from the aching vulnerability of Nemorino in Donizetti's *L'Elisir d'amore* to the larger-than-life passion of Radames in Verdi's *Aïda*. Caruso's fame would far exceed that of Francesco Tamagno and Jean de Reszke, the legendary dramatic tenors who preceded him, and of Alessandro Bonci, the exquisitely refined tenor who was considered his chief rival.

The primary vehicle of Caruso's fame was recorded sound. Tamagno, who created the title role in Verdi's *Otello*, made only a few records before his death, and Jean de Reszke apparently made none. Bonci made a number of records, as did Fernando de Lucia, a stylish Italian tenor who flourished in Europe around the turn of the century. But none of them sound as thrilling, as flesh-and-blood *alive* on records as did Caruso, who made his first recording in a Milan hotel one afternoon in 1902. In her memoirs, the great soprano Rosa Ponselle, who sang often with

Enrico Caruso as Radames *in* Aïda.

Caruso, despaired of the crudeness and distortion of the sound, as well as the musical and stylistic compromises dictated by time constraints, that took away from the miraculous beauty of Caruso's singing as she knew it personally. Yet despite these limitations, so much comes through in his recordings. It is tragic that Caruso died in 1921, when he was only forty-eight, before electrical recording brought a truer aural image to recorded sound.

Alfredo Kraus (right) and Giuseppe Taddei. Kraus made a specialty of lyric tenor roles.

Jules Massenet, Werther (1893). *Poster by Eugène Grasset.*

In the post-Caruso era, a greatly expanded operatic repertoire was in place, widening the spectrum of the tenor voice. In the two decades between Caruso's death and World War II, tenor singing was at its richest and most diverse. Each country produced a full range of superb tenors, as these recordings indicate.

The devastation of World War II changed forever the world that produced this phenomenon. Operas were no longer being written and produced as before, and the international repertoire was essentially frozen. The style of performing became more musically exacting and theatrically compelling. The art of singing, which had always evolved with the music, began to serve the needs of key interpretive artists, particularly conductors and stage directors. Today, singers no longer develop as freely or as naturally. Impresarios and agents prefer their singers slender and attractive, like movie stars. Emerging talents—sometimes minor ones, with pretty faces and nice figures—are forced to bypass experience and head straight for the lime-light. Modern opera houses have become ridiculously large, in order to sell more tickets. Operatic orchestras are encouraged play more loudly for a more brilliant effect, and some conductors have their orchestras tune to a higher pitch to add even more luster. The toll this takes on singers—especially on tenors—is incalculable.

Yet they flourish. The biggest phenomenon in the world of classical music in the early 1990s was the series of "Three Tenors" concerts. Despite the incessant demands of the music business, the world of singing has enjoyed a golden-age rebirth of the *tenore di grazia*. The arrival of a new *heldentenor* or a promising *lirico-dramatico* is news that spreads like wildfire. We need heroes; so we need tenors. That is "this life" Franco Corelli despaired of. It is the dream-come-true that walks a tightrope.

Just listen . . .

The Recordings

1 **Giacomo Puccini:** *Tosca* (Libretto by Luigi Illica and Giuseppe Giacosa)

Act III — "*E lucevan le stelle***"**
Carlo Bergonzi, tenor
Georges Prêtre, conductor, L'Orchestre de la
Conservatoire de Paris

The handsome young painter Mario Cavaradossi is deeply in love with Floria Tosca, a singer who has bewitched Rome at a time when the city is convulsed by the Napoleonic Wars and its quest for liberty from

Carlo Bergonzi as **Cavaradossi** *in* **Tosca.**

repressive rule. Cavaradossi's libertarian sympathies and his love for Tosca bring him to the attention of Baron Scarpia, the cruel prefect of police. Scarpia wants what Cavaradossi has—information and Tosca's favor—and so condemns the painter to death for treasonous activities and then forces Tosca to sleep with him to save the life of her beloved. As dawn breaks on the day he is to die, Cavaradossi recalls his love for Tosca in the aria "*E lucevan le stelle*" ("The stars were shining")—a love that seems even more glorious as death approaches.

2 **Georges Bizet:** *Carmen* (Libretto by Henri Meilhac and Ludovic Halévy)
Act II—"*La fleur que tu m'avais jetée*" (Flower Song)
José Carreras, tenor
Jacques Delacôte, conductor, Orchestra of the Royal Opera House, Covent Garden

A naïve Spanish officer, Don José, falls under the spell of a seductive gypsy, Carmen, who toys with his affections by tossing him a flower. Carmen dupes him and escapes his custody after a fight that lands José in jail. When he is released, José rushes to the faithless Carmen, but, hearing reveille in the distance, he tells her he must leave. Carmen flies into a rage. José silences her in a burst of fury that gives way to the psychotic rapture of the aria known as the *Flower Song*. Here, he reveals to Carmen that the perfume of the flower she tossed him sustained him in jail. Though he cursed her allure, he thought only of seeing her again.

José Carreras

3 Umberto Giordano: *Andrea Chénier*

Act IV—"*Come un bel dì di Maggio*"
Franco Corelli, tenor
Franco Ferraris, conductor

A real historical character, the French poet Andre Chénier (1762-1794), is the inspiration for Giordano's tumultuous late romantic Italian opera. As the French revolution overwhelms the aristocracy, the beautiful Maddalena, daughter of a noble family, falls in love with the freedom-loving Chénier. But another man lusts after her—Carlo Gerard, servant to Maddalena's family who allies himself with the Revolution. Gerard uses intrigue and the violent authority of the Revolution to get rid of Chénier, who is condemned to death. On the morning he is to go to the guillotine, Chénier expresses his profound feelings in the aria "*Come un bel dì di Maggio*" ("Like a beautiful day in May").

4 Gaetano Donizetti: *L'Elisir d'amore* (Libretto by Felice Romani)

Act II—"*Una furtiva lagrima*"
Nicolai Gedda, tenor
Francesco Molinari-Pradelli, conductor, Rome Opera House Orchestra

"The elixir of love" in the title of Donizetti's most popular comedy refers to a potion the young bumpkin Nemorino thinks will make the beautiful Adina fall in love with him. In the opera's second act, he despairs of the tear he saw on Adina's cheek—"*Una furtiva lagrima*" ("A furtive tear"). The anguish he feels for her makes it clear how profoundly he loves her. This aria, which is not particularly high or demanding, is one of the most expressive and revealing for any lyric tenor, a perfect vehicle for the art of *bel canto*.

⑤ Giuseppe Verdi: *Rigoletto* (Libretto by Francesco Maria Piave)

Act IV—*"La donna è mobile"*
Alfredo Kraus, tenor
Julius Rudel, conductor, Philharmonia Orchestra

In the court of the playboy Duke of Mantua, the jester Rigoletto is the king of revelry. The constant, heartless jokes the courtiers play on one another, led by Rigoletto himself, take on special significance when they decide to kidnap the Duke's newest amorous conquest, who, unknown to them, is Rigoletto's daughter, Gilda. When Rigoletto discovers that Gilda has fallen for the Duke, whom she believes is a student, he is so enraged that he plans to kill his master. The plot is set in motion at the riverfront tavern of Sparafucile, where the Duke has gone in search of a woman for the evening. As the Duke waits to meet Sparafucile's sister, Maddalena, he arrogantly sings of the fickleness of women (*"La donna è mobile"*).

John McCormack as **Don Ottavio** *in* **Don Giovanni.**

Wolfgang Amadeus Mozart: *Don Giovanni*

(Libretto by Lorenzo da Ponte)

⑥ **Act I—*"Dalla sua pace"***
Luigi Alva, tenor
Carlo Maria Giulini, conductor, Philharmonia Orchestra

⑦ **Act II, Scene 2—*"Il mio tesoro"***
John McCormack, tenor
Walter Rogers, conductor

Don Ottavio, the tenor role in *Don Giovanni*, is an honorable man in a world where all the other men seem to be libertines or fools. He is in love with Donna Anna, who is seduced by

Pietro Mascagni

the opera's title character, the legendary Don Juan—an act that sets in motion a chain of events, beginning with the murder of Donna Anna's father, that has fateful consequences for everyone. Donna Anna confides in Don Ottavio her suspicions that Don Giovanni may be her father's murderer, and swears revenge. Don Ottavio realizes that everything he desires depends on Donna Anna—"*Dalla sua pace la mia dipende*" ("On her peace of mind, mine depends as well"). In the opera's second act, Don Ottavio vows to those who have been wronged that he will exact satisfaction from Don Giovanni. He bids them find his beloved Donna Anna and take care of her—"*Il mio tesoro intanto andate a consolar*" ("Meanwhile go and console my treasure"). The demands of this aria, with its graceful, long-breathed melodic lines, make it a supreme test of the lyric tenor's art.

⑧ **Pietro Mascagni:** *L'Amico Fritz* (Libretto by Nicola Daspuro)
Act III—"*O amore, o bella luce del core*"
Luciano Pavarotti, tenor
Gianandrea Gavazzeni, conductor, Orchestra of the Royal Opera House, Covent Garden

Best known as the composer of the one-act thriller *Cavalleria Rusticana*, Mascagni (1863–1945) had a turbulent career that lasted a generation longer than that of his conservatory classmate Giacomo Puccini. Mascagni was an international sensation at the age of twenty-seven, when *Cavalleria Rusticana* premiered, though the disappointment that greeted his next opera—the charming *L'Amico Fritz* —foreshadowed the rest of his uneven career. *L'Amico Fritz* is typical: an opera filled with beautiful individual moments and passages that don't add up to much theatrically. The title character's big moment in *L'Amico Fritz* is an impassioned meditation on the agony and ecstasy of love—*"O amore, o bella luce del core!"* ("O love, o radiant light of the heart!")

9 **Giuseppe Verdi:** *Aïda* (Libretto by Antonio Ghislanzoni and Camille du Locle)
Act I—*"Se quel guerrier io fosi . . . Celeste Aïda"*
Richard Tucker, tenor
Tullio Serafin, conductor, Orchestra of Teatro alla Scala, Milan

As war with Ethiopia draws near, a war the Egyptian general Radames hopes he will lead, he dreams of victory and of returning to wed his beloved Aïda, a slave who is the captive daughter of the Ethiopian king. In the aria's stirring recitative, bolstered by fanfares, Radames imagines himself the hero—*"Se quel guerrier io fosi"* ("If I were that warrior"). Turning his thoughts to Aïda, he settles into an ecstatic reverie—*"Celeste Aïda"* ("Heavenly Aïda")—in which he promises to return her to her native land, crown her queen, and build her a throne near the sun.

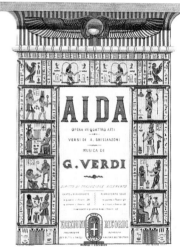

Aida, *Title page of the vocal score, 1872.*

Franco Corelli

10 **Ruggiero Leoncavallo:** *I Pagliacci*

(Libretto by the composer)

Act I—*"Recitar! . . . Vesti la giubba"*
Franco Corelli, tenor
Lovro von Matacic, conductor, Orchestra of Teatro alla Scala, Milan

I Pagliacci (The Clowns) is based on a true story Leoncavallo heard from his father, who was a judge. It tells the sad tale of Canio, the leader of a troupe of comedians performing classic *commedia dell'arte* stage routines. Canio is a neurotic man, jealous of other men's interest in his beautiful young wife, Nedda. He has reason to be jealous: The disfigured clown Tonio lusts after Nedda (who dismisses him), while the handsome Silvio is actually her lover. Tonio overhears their assignation and tells Canio. Shattered, Canio still has to perform—*"Recitar! Mentre preso dal delirio!"* ("Perform the play! While I am wracked with grief!")—and reaches the anguished conclusion that he must perform because he is not a man but a clown. *"Vesti la giubba"* ("Don the costume"), he sings, realizing that the clown must laugh (*"Ridi, Pagliaccio!"*) as his heart breaks.

11 **Francesco Cilea:** *L'Arlesiana* (Libretto by Leopoldo Marenco)

Act II—*"È la solita storia del pastor"*
Giuseppe di Stefano, tenor
Albert Erede, Orchestra of Milan

The international success of *Adriana Lecouvreur* was still five years away for Francesco Cilea when *L'Arlesiana* premiered in 1897. If critics and audiences

Amilcare Ponchielli

were underwhelmed by this pastoral tragedy, they were overwhelmed by the young tenor who debuted the role of Federico—Enrico Caruso. Federico, a simple young shepherd in Provence, is deeply in love with a woman from Arles. When he learns the woman is promiscuous, he is heartbroken. He pours out his wounded feelings in the aria *"È la solita storia del pastore"* ("And that is the shepherd's lonely tale"), a moment of aching vulnerability that demands of the tenor voice infinite tenderness.

12 **Amilcare Ponchielli:** *La Gioconda* (Libretto by Arrigo Boïto)
Act II—*"Cielo e mar"*
Nicolai Gedda, tenor
Giuseppe Patané, conductor, Orchestra of the Royal Opera House, Covent Garden

The gifted Italian composer Amilcare Ponchielli should be more famous than he is—he might have been Verdi's heir—but he died tragically in 1886, at the age of fifty-two. His masterpiece, *La Gioconda*, is a sweeping tale of political and romantic intrigue set in the decadent splendor of seventeenth-century Venice. The complicated plot is built around a street singer known as La Gioconda, who loves Enzo Grimaldo, a sailor and Genoese prince who loves another woman, Laura. In the second act, Enzo passes a moment alone on the deck of his ship, savoring the beauty of the sea and the night sky in the tender aria *"Cielo e mar"* ("Sky and sea"), and longing to have his beloved Laura in his arms again.

13 **Giacomo Puccini:** *Manon Lescaut* (Libretto by Luigi Illica, Giuseppe Giacosa, Giulio Ricordi, Marco Praga, and Domenico Oliva)

Act I—*"Donna non vidi mai"*
Plàcido Domingo, tenor
Bruno Bartoletti, conductor, New Philharmonia Orchestra

Giacomo Puccini's volatile, lusty 1893 opera differs strikingly from French composer Jules Massenet's earlier, elegant *Manon*, also based on the Abbé Prévost's novel. Both tell of the tragic love affair of the coquettish Manon Lescaut and the high-born Chevalier des Grieux. Puccini captures the magic of the moment they meet in a typically forthright manner in the rhapsodic aria *"Donna non vidi mai simile a questa"* ("Never have I seen such a woman"), in which des Grieux daydreams about Manon's beauty.

14 **Edouard Lalo:** *Le roi d'Ys* (Libretto by Edouard Blau)

Act III—*"Puisqu'on ne peut fléchir ces jalouses gardiennes . . . Vainement, ma bien-aimée"*
Beniamino Gigli, tenor
Rainaldo Zamboni, Covent Garden Orchestra

The French composer Edouard Lalo had his greatest operatic success with *Le roi d'Ys*, which premiered in 1888. Based on a Breton legend, the story concerns the soldier, Mylio, who must contend with the affections of both daughters of the King of Ys— Rozenn, whom he loves, and the treacherous

Beniamino Gigli

Margared, who is determined to have him. Rozenn is so distraught by her sister's betrayal that she locks herself in her bedchamber. In a moment of disarming tenderness, Mylio stations himself outside Rozenn's locked door and serenades her in the lilting *"Vainement, ma bien-aimée!"* ("Vainly, my beloved!"), in which he promises to wait as long as necessary for her to emerge and return to his arms.

15 **Charles François Gounod: *Roméo et Juliette*** (Libretto by Jules Barbier and Michel Carré)
Act II—*"Ah! lèves-toi soleil!"*
Jussi Björling, tenor
Nils Grevillius, conductor, Royal Opera House Orchestra, Stockholm

Charles François Gounod

Gounod's opera closely follows William Shakespeare's play, with occasional digressions, plot twists, and characters designed to appeal to the tastes and expectations of nineteenth-century opera audiences. The heart of the opera is the balcony scene. Gounod captures the aching rapture of Romeo and Juliet's blossoming love. In the opera's second act, Romeo is brought to the Capulets' garden, where he is mesmerized by the light streaming from Juliet's window. To his own question, "What sudden light through yonder window breaks?" Romeo answers in the aria *"Ah! lèves-toi, soleil!"* ("Ah, arise, o sun!"), rhapsodizing over Juliet's beauty, which obliterates the stars and the night, and longs for her to appear on the balcony.

16 **Wolfgang Amadeus Mozart:** *Così fan tutte* (Libretto by Lorenzo da Ponte)

Act I, Scene 4— *"Un'aura amorosa"*
Alfredo Kraus, tenor
Karl Böhm, conductor,
Philharmonia Orchestra

Così fan tutte, translated loosely as "So are all women," refers to a cynical bet made in the opera's opening scene. A pair of officers, Ferrando and Guglielmo, wager their bachelor friend, Don Alfonso, that their lovers, the sisters Dorabella and Fiordiligi,

Così fan tutte, *title page, 1790.*

will remain faithful in their absence. Don Alfonso is sure these women will stray, because that is the way all women are. As part of the bet, the officers disguise themselves as Albanian noblemen so that each can woo the other's lover. As he begins this absurd quest with Guglielmo, Ferrando muses on his faith in his precious Dorabella in the gently ardent aria *"Un'aura amorosa"* ("A loving breath").

17 **Ruggiero Leoncavallo: "Mattinata"** (Text by the composer)

Enrico Caruso, tenor
Ruggiero Leoncavallo, piano (recorded 1904)

Though "Mattinata" is a song and not an aria, its timeless melody could fit easily into an opera. Leoncavallo, who wrote the text as well as the music, was a leading Italian operatic composer at the turn of the century who had great success with his one-act opera *I Pagliacci*. His fame was eclipsed by the rise of Puccini, and the embittered Leoncavallo never enjoyed a success to equal his first. He accompanies Caruso at the piano in this priceless recording made in Milan in 1904. "Mattinata," which has been adapted and performed in every conceivable manner as a pop song, is the outpouring of a passionate lover who greets the dawn while his beloved still sleeps. He implores the sleeping one to wake and make their dream of love a radiant reality.

18 **Richard Wagner:** *Tristan und Isolde* (Libretto by the composer)
Act II— *"O König, das kann ich dir nicht sagen"*
Lauritz Melchior, tenor
Robert Heger, conductor, London Symphony Orchestra (recorded 1930)

The epic story of Tristan and Isolde tells of a forbidden love that leaves a trail of human wreckage in the wake of its all-consuming passion. Tristan has been dispatched by his uncle, King Marke of Cornwall, to serve as an escort to the Irish princess Isolde, now betrothed to the king. Their repressed feelings erupt violently when Tristan and Isolde share what turns out to be not poison but a love potion. No longer able to deny their feelings, they meet under the cloak of night and make love with scant concern for the implications of their betrayal. The king is devastated to discover Tristan and Isolde consummating their love, and begs Tristan to explain. In his response *"O König, das kann ich dir nicht sagen"* ("O King, that I cannot tell you"), Tristan says that he has no explanation; he is no longer concerned with anything but his passion. He asks Isolde to follow him into death, that "wondrous realm of night," where their love can find everlasting refuge.

The Tenors

Peruvian-born **Luigi Alva** (b. 1927), a fine example of the *tenore di grazia*, sang with the agility and style that term suggests. Like many singers in

Luigi Alva

Spanish-speaking countries, Alva made his debut in *zarzuela* (a type of Spanish operetta) but quickly established himself in the uniquely demanding lyric tenor roles written by Mozart and Rossini. He never risked the sweetness and smooth beauty of his voice on more forceful roles, though the clarity, range, and elegance of his singing gave him great presence. Much of Alva's career was centered in Europe, both in the leading opera houses and at distinguished summer festivals. He also sang at the Metropolitan Opera.

Carlo Bergonzi (b. 1924) began his singing career as a baritone in 1948 in his native Italy, where he bowed as Figaro in Rossini's *Il barbiere di Siviglia*. His second debut, in 1951, established him as a tenor of great promise and began his remarkable international career. Bergonzi's mellow, handsome voice never offered the trumpeting brilliance of a *tenore di forza* as did those of his contemporaries Franco Corelli and Mario del Monaco, though they often sang the same roles. Bergonzi's singing was instead a model of unfailing sensitivity and refinement, even in vigorous roles such as Radames in *Aïda* or Manrico in *Il Trovatore*. The result was a distinguished career that lasted for almost forty years. Well into his sixties, Bergonzi earned great acclaim at the Metropolitan Opera as the youthful Nemorino in *L'Elisir d'amore*.

Of all the tenors heralded as Caruso's successor, Sweden's **Jussi Björling** (1911–1960) probably came closest to claiming the distinction, according to Caruso's widow. Like Beniamino Gigli, he made an easy transition from boy soprano to lyric tenor (his professional debut came when he was nineteen) without losing the purity of sound he had had as a child. Björling's was a voice of astonishing beauty—even his clarion high notes had a rich, supple sound—backed by a refined musical taste and a solid vocal technique that remains the envy of tenors everywhere. Although he was short and an indifferent actor, the sheer allure of his singing silenced any criticism of his performances. Though it had darkened in color, Björling's voice was virtually undimmed in its luster and flexibility when he died of a heart attack at the age of forty-nine.

One of the indefatigable "Three Tenors," Spain's **José Carreras** (b. 1946) has followed the example of his friend and countryman Plàcido Domingo in pursuing a glamorous and lucrative career as a lyric-dramatic tenor who explores a broad repertoire while taking full advantage of the multimedia potential of modern operatic stardom. At the beginning of his career, Carreras's radiant voice—almost an echo of Gigli's—was a more sensitive and lyric instrument than Domingo's. Consequently his voice lost much of its bloom when he

José Carreras

began to sing *spinto* and dramatic roles. Criticisms of his choice of repertoire had little effect on the remarkable career of this beloved figure, but leukemia nearly ended it in the late 1980s. His heroic return to singing (largely in recitals, concerts, and recordings) after battling the disease gave him a special place in the affections of audiences everywhere.

The twentieth century's most influential opera singer, **Enrico Caruso** (1873–1921), is still astonishingly popular three-quarters of a century after his death at the age of forty-eight. The brilliance and muscular beauty of his voice were unique—particularly in the sumptuous, baritone-like sound of his lower register—when his international career began to develop at the turn of the century. The luxuriant abandon of his singing was matched by his passionate commitment on the stage. With roles such as the Duke in *Rigoletto* and Nemorino in *L'Elisir d'amore*, he created in audiences the kind of hysteria usually reserved for great divas. Caruso possessed the most "phonogenic" voice of his day, and recordings were the source of much of his unprecedented popularity. Made before the invention of the microphone, these recordings betray obvious sonic limitations, but his large, varied catalog of records is priceless evidence of Caruso's artistry. (The recording heard here is one of his earliest.) Mario Lanza's winning performance in the title role of MGM's highly fictionalized film of 1950, *The Great Caruso*, underscored Caruso's continuing influence and inspired a new generation of tenors, including the young José Carreras.

The most volatile and mesmerizing Italian tenor of his generation, **Franco Corelli** (b. 1921) dominated heroic operatic roles in the 1950s and 1960s with his sensuous voice, the wild abandon of his singing, and his striking stage presence. Well over six feet tall and as handsome as a matinee idol, Corelli looked as dashing as he sounded. He had a natural voice of such brilliance that the tenor Giovanni Martinelli once compared Corelli's full-throated singing to the warmth of the Italian sun. Corelli was unforgettable in Verdi's *Aïda*, *Il Trovatore*, and *Don Carlos*, and in *Andrea Chénier*, *I Pagliacci*, and Mascagni's *Cavalleria Rusticana*, as well as the tenor heroes in Puccini's *Tosca*, *La Fanciulla del West*, and *Turandot*. At the Metropolitan Opera—where he made his 1961 debut on the same night as Leontyne Price—he delivered memorable performances as Romeo in Gounod's *Roméo et Juliette* and in the title role of Massenet's *Werther*. Corelli was heavily criticized for the hysteria that marked his singing and stage performances, but his unique intensity was sorely missed when he retired suddenly, while still in good voice, in the early 1970s.

No Italian tenor of the post-World War II era inspires as much affection or frustration as **Giuseppe di Stefano** (b. 1921). In the late 1940s and early 1950s, he sang lyric roles that took full advantage of his sensuous voice and mesmerizing ability to sing softly—live recordings from this period document his ability to trumpet a ringing high C, then file it down to a dazzling pianissimo whisper. Di Stefano's singing also possessed a caressing, erotic quality, a marked departure from the chaste style of his model, Beniamino Gigli. Di Stefano pushed too soon and too relentlessly into heavier repertoire, however. By the late 1950s, his singing had begun to coarsen and lose its flexibility and its sweetness, and his stage career effectively ended in the

Giuseppe di Stefano and Maria Callas

mid-1960s. A thrilling performer, di Stefano is remembered for his recordings as well as for his collaborations with Maria Callas.

Few singers in history have had as comprehensive or impressive a career as **Plàcido Domingo** (b. 1941). Born in Spain but raised in Mexico, where his parents performed in *zarzuela*, Domingo studied piano and conducting before turning to singing. His debut, at sixteen, was as a baritone in *zarzuela*. Within three years he had switched to tenor roles and made a second debut, as Alfredo in *La Traviata*. A shrewd and industrious artist, Domingo apprenticed with the Israel National Opera (singing most performances in Hebrew) while also performing tirelessly in regional American companies and provincial German opera houses. He made his New York City Opera debut in 1966, moving to the Metropolitan Opera two years later. Since then, his international career has been a succession of triumphs, in a mind-boggling spectrum that includes everything from Mozart and *bel canto* to the imposing *heldentenor* roles of Wagner and Strauss. Domingo's superior musical skills enabled him quickly to master this vast repertoire, leading to some criticism about his restless ambition. One of the first latter-day singers to exploit "crossover" success in pop music, Domingo has also pursued a career as a conductor.

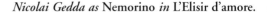

Nicolai Gedda as Nemorino *in* L'Elisir d'amore.

The finest example of the cosmopolitan modern tenor, **Nicolai Gedda** (b. 1925) defies classification by either voice type or nationality—a lyric tenor who had enduring success in heavier roles, a Swede who was a paragon of style singing in French, Russian, and English. Gedda spent his early childhood in Leipzig, but returned to Sweden, where he began vocal studies. His 1951 debut at the Royal Stockholm Opera, in Adam's *Le Postillon du Longjumeau*, showcased the ringing, lyric beauty of his voice and brilliant top register. The following year, Walter Legge of EMI signed him, beginning a prodigious recording career that lasted more than forty years. Gedda's unparalleled command of languages gave him an authority in repertoire other tenors avoided. His superb technique, which he constantly refined, kept his voice in remarkable shape well into his sixties. The intelligence and assurance with which Gedda applied his gifts made him equally at home in Verdi's *Rigoletto*, Massenet's *Werther*, and Tchaikovsky's *Eugene Onegin*, as well as in Viennese operetta, the Passion music of Bach, and an infinite variety of song and concert music.

Perhaps the sweetest lyric tenor voice belonged to **Beniamino Gigli** (1890–1957). A choirboy in his youth, he eventually won a scholarship to Rome's Liceo Musicale di Santa Cecilia. When Gigli won a singing competition in 1914, one of the judges, Caruso's great tenor rival Alessandro Bonci, wrote

Beniamino Gigli

in his notes, "At last we have found *the* Tenor." The young tenor's professional operatic debut soon followed, and his velvety singing reminded Italian audiences of the young Caruso. Caruso's eventually fatal illness led the Metropolitan Opera to engage Gigli, and he continued to sing there, assuming most of Caruso's roles, until a salary dispute during the Great Depression. The rest of Gigli's career was spent in South America and Europe, with a brief return to New York in the late 1930s. He was exceptionally selective about using his gentle, lyric voice in heavier repertoire, which sustained its high quality throughout his long career. Gigli's taste was questionable at times—he would resort to corny emotional effects, such as sobbing, and sometimes blithely disregarded style—but the sheer beauty and ease of his singing, as well as his innate sense of the line of the music, are still something to behold.

At an age when most tenors were fondly recalling the days when they could easily claim high Cs, **Alfredo Kraus** (b. 1927) was still singing them in the world's great opera houses. Born in the Canary Islands, he made his debut in 1951 in Cairo as the Duke in *Rigoletto*, a demanding lyric role that became a constant throughout his career. Kraus made a wise decision early on—he carefully selected roles he liked and could sing well and stuck with them, resisting the temptation to push his voice beyond its limits. They are demanding roles:

Gounod's Faust and Roméo, the title role in *Werther*, Alfredo in *La Traviata*, Ferrando in *Così fan tutte*, Hoffmann in *Les contes d'Hoffmann*, and Tonio and the Duke in *La fille du regiment*. With age Kraus's artistry only deepened, and his career enjoyed a resurgence beginning in the late 1970s. In an age of reckless career choices by colleagues, his operatic performances set a distinctive standard of technical refinement and impeccable subtlety.

Born and trained in Dublin, the tenor **John McCormack** (1884–1945) was an opera singer of great skill and refinement. He also studied in Italy, where he made his operatic debut under the name Giovanni Foli. Opera audiences in New York and London acclaimed his performances in lyric roles, while the phenomenal popularity of his concert appearances rivaled that of Caruso's. Recordings testify to the quality of his singing—his version of Mozart's "*Il mio tesoro*" heard here is considered a benchmark for the aria—and the lyric beauty of his voice was unique, even in a golden age of tenor singing. Uncomfortable as an actor, McCormack began to shift the emphasis of his career to concert work, particularly Irish and sentimental songs, which he sang with haunting style and consummate taste. Performing infrequently in opera after World War I, he became an American citizen in 1919, appeared in movies, and received a knighthood from the Pope. After a farewell concert in London in 1938, he spent the rest of his life in his native Ireland.

The Danish tenor **Lauritz Melchior** (1890–1973) exemplifies the Wagner *heldentenor.* His singing delivered the power and stamina Wagner demanded in a tonally rich, heroic voice. Melchior was a baritone when he began his singing career in 1913 in Copenhagen. His second debut, in 1924, announced the arrival of the consummate Wagnerian tenor. Melchior was engaged that year for

Lauritz Melchior as **Tannhäuser.**

the Bayreuth Festival, where he studied the Wagner repertoire with the composer's son. A great bear of a man and an instinctive artist, Melchior horrified purists by arguing for cuts in Wagner's long operas, though the quality of his singing more than balanced those concerns. Melchior also enjoyed concert and movie work. His willingness to indulge in the tackier side of show business so appalled Sir Rudolf Bing that it led to Melchior's departure from the Metropolitan Opera. Since his retirement, tenors have struggled in vain to equal the power and splendor of his singing of Wagner.

Not since Caruso has a tenor enjoyed such sweeping popularity as has **Luciano Pavarotti** (b. 1935). A huge man with a thoroughly ingratiating manner, Pavarotti had a lucky break as a young lyric tenor, when soprano Joan Sutherland and her husband, conductor Richard Bonynge, signed him to sing in an opera company they organized to tour Australia in 1965. He had already sung in Italy and at England's Glyndebourne Festival, but the company gave him the opportunity to explore the *bel canto* literature with the soprano as his partner. When he appeared with Sutherland in Donizetti's *La fille du regiment* at Covent Garden and the Metropolitan Opera, as well as in a best-selling recording, Pavarotti established himself as a crowd-pleasing tenor in that opera's notorious aria with nine high Cs. He is perhaps the last in a long line of great Italian lyric tenors, a singer of distinctive taste and charm. His voice lacks the honeyed quality of Gigli's, but its passionate, edgier sound has allowed him to sing heavier roles, even the title role in Verdi's *Otello*. Along with his colleague and sometimes rival Plàcido Domingo, Pavarotti has dominated the lyric-dramatic tenor repertoire in the last third of the twentieth century.

American-born tenors have been popular and admired for several decades, but none of them has had the staying power of **Richard Tucker** (1913–1975). He was one of the last singers to be strongly identified with one opera house—New York's Metropolitan Opera—and it became the foundation of his international success. Born Reuben Ticker, Tucker began singing in synagogue and studied voice with the dramatic tenor Paul Althouse while working in the garment business. A concert engagement in New York quickly led to his Metropolitan Opera debut in 1945 and, along with his brother-in-law Jan Peerce, he became a mainstay of the company's roster for the rest of his career. His voice benefited from his experience in singing Jewish liturgical music, and his sturdy technique assured him of a long and satisfying career. Though Tucker was not a particularly subtle or debonair singer—Franco Corelli sang many of the same roles with greater variety and texture—he was a dependable and passionate one, with a great voice that was perfect for the heroic lyric-dramatic roles in the operas of Verdi and Puccini. Even people who knew little about opera loved Tucker, whose congenial public personality and lack of pretense made him an especially accessible opera star. Characteristically, his generosity extended beyond his sudden death, when his family established the Richard Tucker Foundation, which encourages the careers of young singers and presents what has become the most important singing prize given in the United States.

CREDITS:

The Pierpont Morgan Library/Art Resource, NY: 28; The Bettmann Archive: Cover, 3, 12, 18, 24, 46; Dover Publications, Inc.: 15, 21, 22, 27, 30, 31, 32, 33, 37, 39; 41, 43, 45; EMI Records, Ltd.: 11, 14, 16, 29; EMI Records, Ltd./Photo by G. MacDomnic: 20, 35; OPERA NEWS/The Metropolitan Opera: 17; Louis Mélançon/OPERA NEWS, The Metropolitan Opera Guild: 23, 40; E.F. Foley/OPERA NEWS, The Metropolitan Opera Guild: 26.

Richard Tucker